Water & The Forest Service

James Sedell, **National Interdeputy Water Coordinator, PNW**
Maitland Sharpe, **Policy Analysis, WO**
Daina Dravnieks Apple, **Policy Analysis, WO**
Max Copenhagen, **Watershed and Air, WO**
Mike Furniss, **Rocky Mountain Research Station, Stream Systems Technology Center**

Contributors:

Mike Ash	Engineering, WO
Enoch Bell	Pacific Southwest Research Station
Tom Brown	Rocky Mountain Research Station
Dave Cross	Wildlife, Fish, and Rare Plants, WO
Ed Dickerhoof	Resource Valuation and Use Research, WO
Mary Ellen Dix	Forest Health Protection, WO
Steve Glasser	Watershed and Air, WO
Dave Hohler	Pacific Northwest Research Station
Jim Keys	Watershed and Air, WO
Russ LaFayette	Watershed and Air, WO
Keith McLaughlin	Watershed and Air, WO
John Nordin	Cooperative Forestry, WO
Doug Ryan	Wildlife, Fish, and Watershed Research, WO
Larry Schmidt	Rocky Mountain Research Station, Stream Systems Technology Center
Rick Swanson	Watershed and Air, WO
Paul Tittman	Lands, WO

USDA Forest Service
Policy Analysis
P.O. Box 96090
Washington, DC 20090-6090

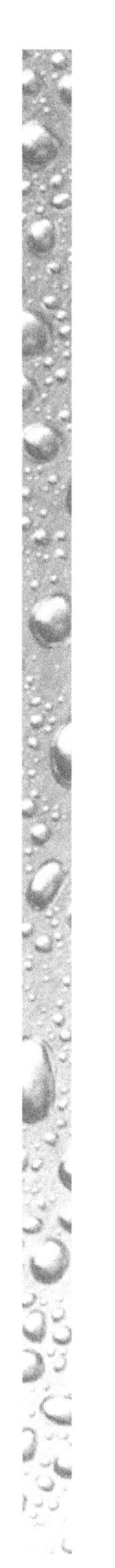

Contents

Summary

Public concern about adequate supplies of clean water led to the establishment in 1891 of federally protected forest reserves. The Forest Service Natural Resources Agenda is refocusing the agency on its original purpose.

This report focuses on the role of forests in water supply—including quantity, quality, timing of release, flood reductions and low flow augmentation, economic value of water from national forest lands, and economic benefits of tree cover for stormwater reduction in urban areas.

Healthy Forests are Vital to Clean Water

Forests are key to clean water. About 80 percent of the Nation's scarce freshwater resources originate on forests, which cover about one-third of the Nation's land area. The forested land absorbs rain, refills underground aquifers, cools and cleanses water, slows storm runoff, reduces flooding, sustains watershed stability and resilience, and provides critical habitat for fish and wildlife. In addition to these ecological services, forests provide abundant water-based recreation and other benefits that improve the quality of life.

Maintaining and Restoring Watersheds were Primary Reasons for Establishing the National Forests

Use and development of the water resources of the United States underwent major changes during the 19th century in response to the growing demands of a population that had increased nearly 20-fold since the founding of the country. Westward expansion, and navigable rivers, canals, and harbors for transportation transformed the Nation's economy. As the Nation experienced this period of massive development, major problems emerged from overuse and poor management of its water resources:

- Urban water supplies were a major source of disease.
- The capacity of many lakes and streams to assimilate wastes was exceeded.
- The survival of people living in arid or flood-prone areas depended on unpredictable precipitation patterns.

The 1897 Organic Administrative Act said these forest reserves were to protect and enhance water supplies, reduce flooding, secure favorable conditions of water flow, protect the forest from fires and depredations, and provide a continuous supply of timber

By 1915, national forests in the West had been established in much the form they retain today. These national forests, which included 162 million acres in 1915, were essentially carved out of the public domain. At that time, few Federal forests were designated in the East because of the lack of public domain. Public demands for eastern national forests resulted in passage of the 1911 Weeks Act, authorizing the acquisition of Federal lands to protect the watersheds of navigable streams. From 1911 to 1945, about 24 million acres of depleted farmsteads, stumpfields, and burned woodlands were incorporated into the eastern part of the National Forest System.

This report focuses on the role of forests in water supply—including quantity, quality, timing of release, flood reductions and low flow augmentation, economic value of water from national forest lands, and economic benefits of tree cover for stormwater reduction in urban areas.

Water is the Central Organizer of Ecosystems

Throughout human history, water has played a central, defining role. It has sculpted the biological and physical landscape through erosion and disturbance. The amount, place, and timing of water are reflected in the vegetative mosaic across the landscape. Water has also played a key role in shaping the pattern and type of human occupancy; routes of travel and transportation, patterns of settlement, and the nature and scope of human land-use all owe their characteristics largely to water regimes.

Conversely, social demands on the water resource system have produced major effects on virtually every aspect of that system including quality, quantity, distribution, and form (for example, white water vs. impoundments).

The human uses and values of water shape how it is managed, and the biological and physical characteristics of water shape human values and uses. Thus, water resource management requires a systems approach that includes not only all of the constituent parts, but also the links, relations, interactions, consequences, and implications among these parts.

Traditionally, water has been valued as an engine of development and as the source of commodity and utilitarian values to society. It has sustained agricultural

Summary

production, grown forests, and powered cities and industries. Today, these values remain, but they have been joined by a variety of others. Water is the basis for many of the recreational and amenity values people seek. Increasingly, science shows, and managers recognize, the key role of water flow regimes in ecosystem function and processes. Adequate flow and water quality are essential to maintaining key fish species and fisheries, which in turn, are sources of many economic, cultural, and spiritual values.

Across the Nation, significant challenges to resource managers, scientists, and citizens are presented by emerging conflicts over providing high-quality, abundant flows of water to sustain a burgeoning population, an agricultural industry, historic salmon runs, and populations of other threatened aquatic species.

QUESTIONS ABOUT THE ROLE OF FORESTS IN WATER SUPPLY

How Much Water Comes from the National Forests?

Excluding Alaska, about two-thirds of the Nation's runoff comes from forested areas. National forest lands contribute 14 percent of the total runoff. National forest lands are the largest single source of water in the United States and contribute water of high quality. More than 60 percent of the Nation's runoff is from east of the Mississippi River, where 70 percent of the Nation's private and State forests are located. National forests in the East are responsible for 6 percent of this runoff. National forests in the West provide proportionately more water (33 percent) because they include the headwaters of major rivers and forested areas of major mountain ranges. Forest Service literature from the 1940's to the present has claimed that 50 to 70 percent of the Nation's runoff comes from national forest lands. It is now clear that those claims are overstated.

What is the Value of Water from National Forest Lands?

We calculate the marginal value of water from all national forest lands to equal at least $3.7 billion per year. Annual value of water from national forest lands is greatest in the Pacific Northwest and Pacific Southwest Regions, and lowest in the Southwest Region. These values represent a lower limit on the range of values attributable to waters flowing from the national

forests. The actual values of this water yield are almost certainly higher, but how much higher is not known.

How Should Municipal Watersheds be Managed?

One issue is whether municipal watersheds should be placed under active or passive management regimes to sustain supplies of high-quality water over the long run. Many Forest Service specialists think that water supplies can be best protected by actively managing these watersheds to maintain forest vegetation and watershed processes within their natural range of variation. Conversely, many people in urban centers believe that, in the interest of water quality and safety, people should not alter watersheds in any way, other than to divert the water. Scientific evidence indicates that watersheds can be effectively managed for safe, high-quality water and still provide other resource outputs as byproducts.

Can Forests be Managed to Improve Stream Flow?

Flooding and sedimentation from cutover lands was one of the primary reasons for establishing national forests. The timing of water yields was also an important issue, especially the desire to augment late-season flows.

Vegetative cover and on-site control measures effectively reduce flood peaks. However, significant shifts in the timing of late-season runoff are not likely to be achieved through managing forest vegetation and snow across national forest lands. Treatments that restore slopes, meadows, and channels; increase the routing time between precipitation and runoff; and recharge ground waters can be expected to have a greater effect in sustaining late-season flows.

Although theory suggests that vegetation management can produce more streamflow, for a variety of reasons, general water-yield increases through forest management are likely to fall in an undetectable range. The data suggest that relying on augmentation from national forests will not be a viable strategy for dealing with water shortages. Greater gains can be made by reducing water consumption, improving conservation, and establishing water markets to allocate scarce supplies more efficiently. Providing cold, clear waters of high quality for aquatic organisms and human use is probably the proper focus for managing water on the National Forest System. There is relatively little management can do to increase total water yield, but forest management can have major effects on water quality—affecting temperature, nutrient loadings, sediment yields, and toxic contaminants.

What is the Agency's Role in Protecting Instream Flow and Ground Water?

The Forest Service must actively participate in the processes that allocate surface water, ground water, and water rights. To be effective, this participation must be timely and of impeccable technical quality.

Three needs stand out:

- Forest plan revisions should incorporate instream flow needs to maintain public values. When a State undertakes a basin-wide adjudication of water rights, all beneficial consumptive and instream water uses on national forest lands should be claimed in accordance with State and Federal laws.
- Early and intensive collaboration among existing and potential water users is likely to be the most effective approach. Public and interagency collaboration in forest planning has great potential for solving problems and achieving acceptable solutions, lessening the costly litigation common to water rights issues.
- In many places, the Forest Service lacks the technical expertise in hydrology needed to protect instream flows. Our present workforce of in-house expertise must be conserved and enhanced if costly failures are to be avoided.

What is the Agency's Role in Hydroelectric Relicensing?

From the 1940's to the 1960's, 325 hydroelectric projects were licensed and built on the national forests. These facilities have provided power and recreation for the Nation. However, many of these projects have also had significant adverse effects on national forest resources.

During the next 10 years, more than 180 of these projects come up for relicensing. The relicensing process presents the only opportunity for the Forest Service to address resource damage, mitigate future adverse effects, and significantly influence how these projects will operate for the next 30 to 50 years.

Forest Service participation in the relicensing process could strengthen mitigation and restoration programs on national forest lands that would lead to improved aquatic habitats and increased water quality. Estimates of these benefits to national forest lands exceed a billion dollars. Potential benefits include new and upgraded recreational facilities, restored instream flow regimes, and enhanced habitats for aquatic and terrestrial wildlife. The relicensing effort offers a cost-effective, immediate means to address the goals outlined in the Natural Resources Agenda and Clean Water Action Plan.

What is the Agency's Role in Conserving Aquatic Biodiversity?

National forest lands and waters play a pivotal role in anchoring aquatic species and maintaining biodiversity. More then one-third of national forest lands have been identified as important to maintaining aquatic biodiversity. Five recent, large-scale, ecosystem-based Forest Service assessments identified networks of aquatic conservation watersheds: the Northwest Forest Plan, the Interior Columbia Basin Ecosystem Management Project, the Tongass National Forest Land Management Plan, the Sierra Nevada Framework Project, and the Southern Appalachians Assessment. Such a commitment and a special effort of lands to the purposes of aquatic species conservation could be regarded as the core of the national forest aquatic and biodiversity conservation strategy.

Can the Watershed Condition on National Forests be Restored?

The most comprehensive landscape-scale assessment to date—the Interior Columbia Basin Assessment—found that the momentum from past events will push the system further from the desired condition over the decades to come. Even with aggressive management, that momentum will not be overcome within the next 100 years under projected funding. Progress toward forest health restoration can be expected to proceed very slowly. In the interim, vegetative composition and structure at the landscape scale will be determined by unnaturally large, high-intensity fires. These findings suggest that it will not be feasible to restore all degraded areas. We will have to strategically focus restoration efforts on selected watersheds where we can hope to make a meaningful difference.

What is the Role of Urban Forests in Water Supply?

Counties classified as "urban" contain one-quarter of the total tree cover of the coterminous United States. Urban trees affect water quantity by intercepting precipitation, increasing water infiltration rates, and transpiring water. They can materially reduce the rate and volume of storm water runoff, flood damage, stormwater treatment costs, and other problems related to water quality.

Summary

The Agency Challenge.

The challenge for the Forest Service will be to simultaneously perform the following:

- Systematically restore damaged watersheds on the national forests.
- Mitigate additional watershed damage from land uses and the inevitable major wildfires.
- Foster partnership efforts to meet the most pressing watershed restoration needs when they fall outside of national forest boundaries.

ISSUES AND POLICY

Maintaining supplies of clean water and protecting watersheds were major reasons why public domain forests and rangelands were reserved. It was the headwaters of the western rivers, and cutover and eroded lands in the East, that became the National Forest System. With passage of environmental laws, such as the Clean Water Act and Endangered Species Act, clear standards for water quality were set by Federal and State agencies. Despite water quality improvements resulting from applying these standards, many streams in the Nation are still highly altered from their natural cycles. Under human influences, neither the range of natural conditions nor the full expression of ecological interactions between aquatic and terrestrial ecosystems is permitted.

Many factors affect water quality, production, and quantity. The national population will nearly double within the next 50 years. America's population is getting older, more ethnically diverse, and concentrated in urban areas. The population of the West has increased 50 percent in the last 20 years and is expected to increase another 300 percent by 2040. Much of the West was unproductive as farmland until lands began to be irrigated in the late 1930's. As a result of population growth, large-scale reliance on irrigation, and a host of other factors that have increased water use, water in western streams is generally over appro-

Figure 1. National forest watersheds integrate multiple processes and issues that must be considered in aggregate. Isolated, single-issue solutions won't work.

priated (Moody 1990, NRC 1992). In Oregon and Washington, 40 to 90 percent of the land areas of individual national forests west of the Cascade Range crest are in municipal watersheds. The population surge in the West is increasing the diversion and consumption use of water and, at the same time, demand for water-based recreation (Brown et al. 1991).

This trend will continue and intensify. Most recreation in national forests is associated with some body of water (lakes, reservoirs, or streams). Recent publications (Gillian and Brown 1998) have more closely linked instream-flow issues to recreational activities and have described the complex relationships of recreation uses and water. For example, even without incorporating many of the economic facets of the recreational uses documented in the arid West, the value of instream flows for recreational fishing is greater than the value of that water for irrigation (Hansen and Hallam 1990).

There are more than 180 non-Federal dams on national forests that provide hydroelectricity as well as recreation. These dams are due for relicensing in the next 5 to 10 years. The Forest Service, under the Federal Power Act of 1920, is legally bound to condition the licenses to mitigate the effects of these dams on fish, wildlife, water quality, and recreation values.

The Nature Conservancy (1996) and other recent assessments have described the deteriorating condition of freshwater species and ecosystems in the United States. More than 300 freshwater species are listed or proposed for listing under the Endangered Species Act. More than 37 percent of native fish species are at risk of extinction, including all of the major populations of salmon and steelhead trout on the west coast south of Alaska. National forest lands contain the best habitat and strongest remaining populations of most of the species at risk. The Nature Conservancy estimated that protecting and restoring 327 watersheds (~800,000 acres each) or 15 percent of the total number of subbasins in the United States would conserve populations of all at-risk freshwater fish and mussel

species in the country. National forest lands influence 181 of these watersheds and will be the anchoring habitat for nearly all of the west coast salmon and trout populations.

INTERPLAY AMONG ISSUES

In addition to the agency's need to consider each of these issues independently, the interplay among them must also be considered (see figure 1). For instance, many of the reservoirs in national forests were built to meet many different needs, including water for agriculture. On the west side of the Oregon Cascades, only 5 percent of the water that agricultural water rights holders are entitled to has been claimed. If they begin to claim more of their entitlement, flows, water quantity, and recreation will likely be affected in major ways. Moreover, several species of salmonids already listed under the Endangered Species Act need more water in certain locales. Recognizing the loss of natural function and natural hydrologic regimes in these highly altered streams, the Forest Service has been pursuing Federal water rights and adjusting conditions in special-use permits to require bypass-flows. Changes of the status quo in water appropriation deeply concern western State governments and senior water-rights holders. Regional climate shifts and global climate change could further exacerbate these issues and confound them with other water issues.

Various Federal interagency water initiatives are addressing aspects of these issues. But, to date, there has been no effort to characterize the particular role of national forest lands in supplying the Nation's water, or to define the role of Federal lands and water in the matrix of State and private lands.

The Nation's water resources face growing scientific, management, and political challenges. The Forest Service will play a major role in these discussions, improving the ability of policymakers, managers, and citizens to develop options, anticipate consequences and implications, and fashion responsive, informed programs. ❖

Water Quantity and the National Forests

WORLD WATER SUPPLY

Although 70 percent of the Earth's surface is covered with water, the amount of fresh water available on land surfaces is a tiny fraction of the total; 97.5 percent of the water on the planet is in the oceans — too salty to drink or to grow crops. Most of the 2.5 percent that is not salt water is locked up out of practical reach in the vast icecaps of Greenland and Antarctica. Less than 1 percent is fresh water, present in the form of groundwater, on the land surface, and in the atmosphere. Less than eight ten-thousandths of 1 percent is annually renewable and available in rivers and lakes for human use including agriculture, and for use by aquatic species (see figure 2).

Water is continuously cycled between the Earth's surface and atmosphere through evaporation and precipitation. The fresh water that falls on land as rain or snow, or that has been accumulated and stored over thousands of years as groundwater, is what people use to meet most of their needs. That supply, although replenished daily, is both limited and vulnerable to human actions and abuse. Over-appropriated rivers and excessive groundwater pumping are serious problems. Many of America's important food-producing regions are sustained by the hydrologic equivalent of deficit financing—using water that is not being replaced. The rational use and protection of water resources are among today's most acute and complex scientific and technical problems. Shortages of fresh water and the increasing pollution of water bodies are becoming limiting factors in the economic development of many countries, even countries not in arid zones. Under these conditions, assessing and managing water resources is vital. Reliable estimates of annual streamflows, their fluctuations, and water resources stored in lakes, aquifers, snowpack, and glaciers are critical to a clear understanding of natural water cycles and the effects of human activities.

All types of waters are renewed, but the rates of renewal differ sharply. Water in rivers is completely renewed every 16 days on average, and water in the atmosphere is renewed every 8 days, but the renewal periods of glaciers, groundwater, ocean water, and the largest lakes run to hundreds or thousands of years. These are, essentially, nonrenewable resources. When people use or degrade these water supplies, useable water resources are lost and natural water cycles may be disrupted.

Figure 2. Only a miniscule proportion of the Earth's water is fresh and available to humans and terrestrial and freshwater aquatic life, making it a most precious resource.

97.5%
Oceans & Seas

1.73%
Glaciers & Icecaps

0.77%
Total Fresh Water

0.0008%
Available & Renewable Fresh Water

Water Quantity and the National Forests

THE QUANTITY OF WATER FROM FORESTED LANDS

Forest Service literature from the 1940's to the present (Gillian and Brown 1998) has asserted that 50 to 70 percent of the Nation's runoff derives from national forest lands. But that assertion is only an often repeated estimate, without a clear empirical basis. More accurate knowledge of how much water comes off national forest lands, where it flows, and how it is used is essential for understanding what waters forest managers are managing, their economic values, and the options for their future use.

In order to answer the fundamental questions about yield and value of waters flowing from the national forests, we estimated runoff using a sophisticated, spatially explicit simulation model. The model found that water yields from national forests are less

Figure 3. Proportion of runoff from all forested lands and national forest of the continental United States (upper graph), derived from Neilson. 1995. Proportion of runoff from all forested lands and national forest lands east and west of the Mississippi River (lower graph).

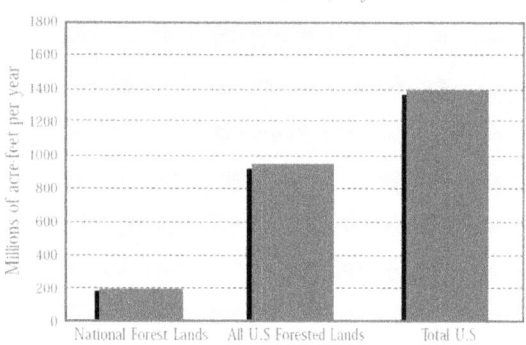

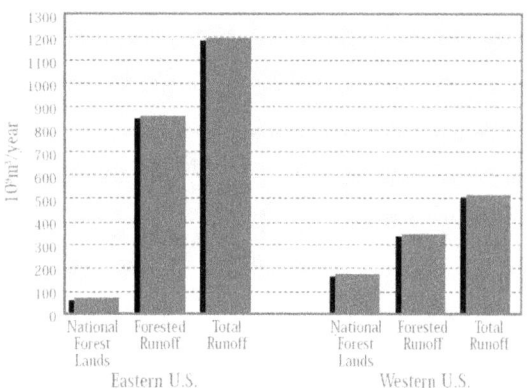

than 20 perent of the total surface runoff from the contiguous 48 States (see figure 3). This is significantly below the estimates of water yield found in earlier Forest Service literature.

Water runoff from forested areas, including national forests, was derived using the Mapped Atmosphere Plant-Soil-System (MAPSS) model (Neilson 1995). The MAPSS model simulates the distribution of forests, savannas, grasslands, and deserts with reasonable accuracy. It is more accurate for forested than nonforested areas, and confidence is lower in the topographically complex and arid Western States. The model produced annual estimates of runoff per 100-square-kilometer grid cell in the continental United States. Forested areas, national forest lands, and watershed boundaries were overlaid on this grid to estimate runoff. In addition, runoff was estimated for the national forests in each of the 18 water-resource regions in the contiguous 48 States.

The model accurately reproduces observed monthly runoff. At the continental and hydrographic-region scales, the model performs well compared to published maps and U.S. Geological Survey data on measured runoff.

About two-thirds of the Nation's runoff, excluding Alaska, comes from forested areas. National forest lands, which represent 8 percent of the contiguous U.S. land area, contribute 14 percent of the runoff. National forest lands are the largest single source of water in the United States. National forests yield water of unusually high quality. This high quality water and its associated watersheds anchor native fishes, mussels, and amphibians. Forested watersheds east of the Mississippi River generally receive more rainfall and produce more surface water per unit area than forested lands to the west. They also tend to have a more even distribution of runoff during the year. Their floods are usually caused by hurricanes or tropical storms, unlike western watersheds in the snow zone where spring snowmelt, sometimes supplemented by rainfall, causes the annual peak flows. Low flows in the East usually occur during dry summers when evapotranspiration rates are greatest; in the western mountains, annual low flows usually occur in midwinter. More than 60 percent of the Nation's runoff is from east of the Mississippi River, where 70 percent of the Nation's private and State forests are located. National forests in the East are responsible for 6 percent of this runoff (see the lower graph in figure 3).

We estimated the actual runoff from national forest lands for the 18 water resource regions of the contiguous United States (see figures 4 and 5). The greatest yield of water from national forest lands is from the Pacific Northwest (Columbia River plus coastal and Puget Sound rivers) and California. These regions have more than 20 percent of their area in national forest lands. The Tennessee River basin has about 6 percent national forest lands, but these are the wettest parts of the basin and yield much more water than their land area would suggest. Although water from national forest land contributes only 6 percent of the Missouri River, it is most of the water from Wyoming, Montana, and Colorado. Nearly half of the water from the Upper Colorado basin flows from national forest lands, yet it yields only about half the water a smaller area of national forest land produces in the Ohio River basin.

Figure 4. Water resources regions of the United States (Source U.S. Geologic Survey). 1 New England; 2 Mid-Atlantic; 3 South Atlantic-Gulf; 4 Great Lakes; 5 Ohio; 6 Tennessee; 7 Upper Mississippi; 8 Lower Mississippi; 9 Souris-Red-Rainy; 10 Missouri; 11 Arkansas-White-Red; 12 Texas Gulf; 13 Rio Grande; 14 Upper Colorado; 15 Lower Colorado; 16 Great Basin; 17 Pacific Northwest; 18 California; 19 Alaska; 20 Hawaii; 21 Puerto Rico.

Figure 5. The contribution and proportion of water runoff from national forest lands to the 18 water resource regions of the contiguous United States. Runoff estimate was derived using the MAPPS model (Neilsen 1995). The bars represent yearly water yields from national forest lands. Percentages are the proportion of the total runoff from the water resource region that flows from national forest lands.

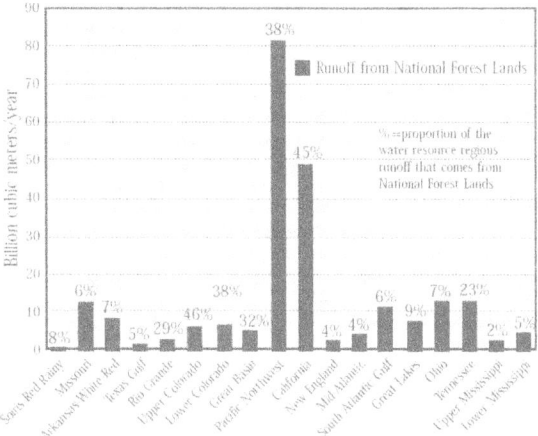

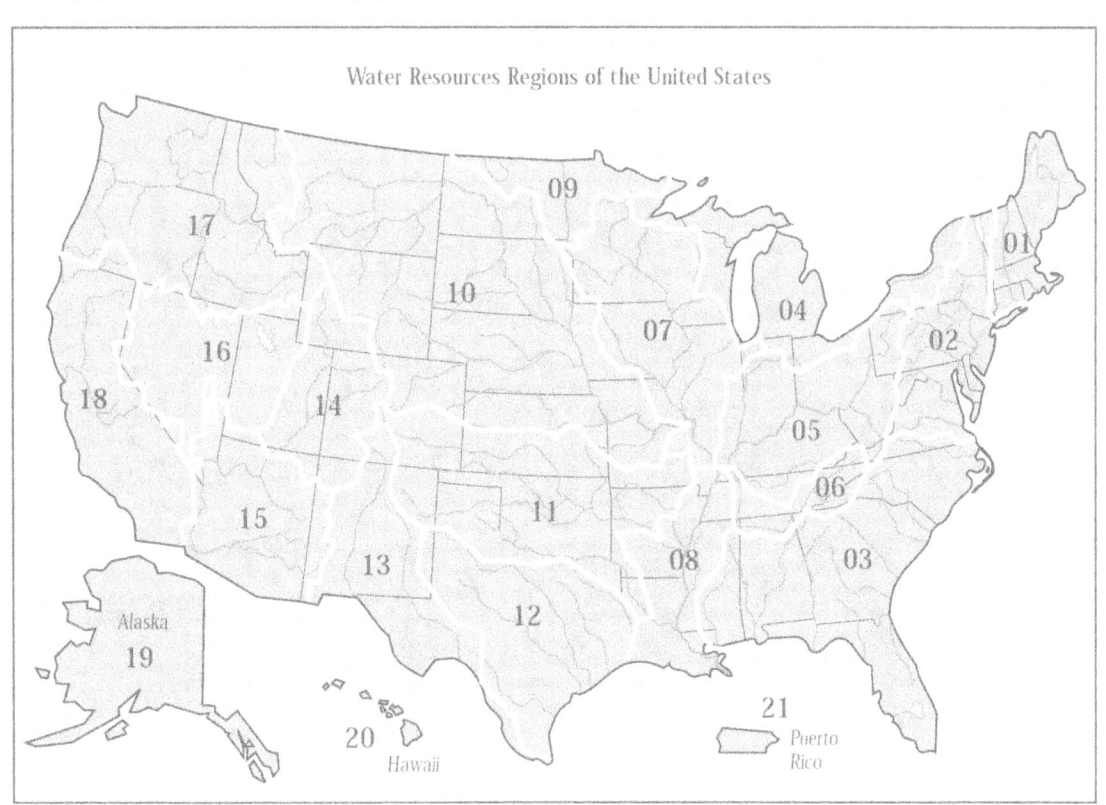

Water Resources Regions of the United States

Water Quantity and the National Forests

National forests in the West provide proportionally more water (33 percent) because they include the major mountain ranges and the headwaters of the principal rivers. For example, in California, national forest lands occupy 20 percent of the State but produce nearly 50 percent of the State's runoff. The Pacific Northwest shows the same pattern.

The agency is using basins and watersheds in the latest rounds of forest plan revisions, regional environmental impact statements, and assessments. Because of higher rainfall in the East, the smaller and more fragmented national forest lands in the Eastern and Southern Regions generate large volumes of runoff compared to the contiguous mountain forests in the Rocky Mountain, Southwest, and Intermountain Regions (see figures 6 and 7). The runoff from the regions provided the basis for calculating the marginal value of water discussed in the next section.

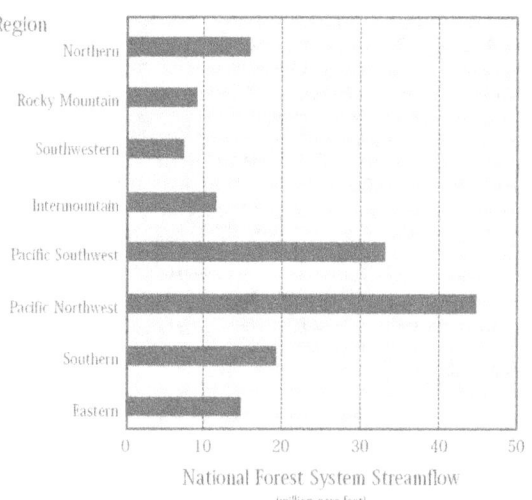

Figure 7. Stream flows from national forest lands for each region. Because of the greater rainfall in the Eastern and Southern United States, more streamflow per unit area comes from these national forests.

Figure 6. The Forest Service has eight administrative regions in the continental United States. The boundaries do not match up well to watersheds or water resource regions.

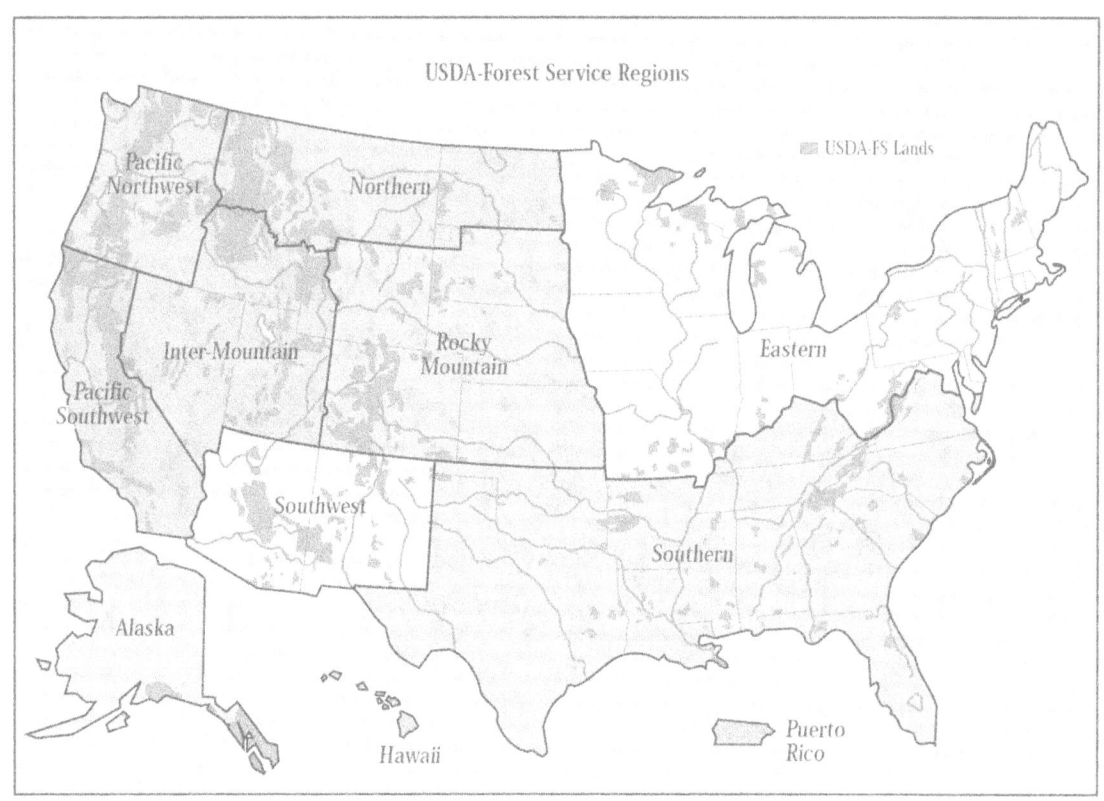

Comparing water supplies to current withdrawals indicates the likelihood that a small change in flow would affect off-stream uses. If only a small proportion of available flow is diverted, off-stream users are unlikely to be affected by a small change in flow, except perhaps in a very dry year. This comparison was performed for the 18 water-resource regions of the contiguous 48 States, with the exception that the upper and lower Colorado regions were combined because so much of the lower basin's supply originates in the upper basin. The proportion of water supply in each region withdrawn for off-stream use is shown in figure 8. In general, off-stream users in regions with ratios below about 0.2 are not likely to be affected by a marginal change in flow. But these regions are large and areas of shortage may exist even in regions with very low total ratios of withdrawal to supply.

Even though the MAPSS model is biased toward underestimating runoff, water yields from national forests are much lower than the estimates that appear in the reports of the Chief dating back to 1947. The figures reported here are more accurate but not precise enough to use on a forest-by-forest basis. Additional work is needed to refine the estimates to the national forest scale.

DETERMINING A WATER VALUE FOR THE NATIONAL FOREST SYSTEM

The economic importance of water can be characterized in two ways, by estimating its economic effects in terms of jobs or income, and by estimating what the public is willing to pay for it. Willingness to pay, the value addressed here, can exist for anything of value—a market good like bottled water, a nonmarket good like a recreational fishing experience, or a so-called "nonuse" service like the knowledge that a certain riparian habitat is well cared for. Measuring these values is anything but straightforward, and most estimates are only approximate.

Most economic valuation studies of water have focused on the marginal value of water volumes available for instream and offstream uses. The estimated marginal values reflect our willingness to pay for a change in the amount of water, and they are of interest because management actions typically cause only small changes. In some water-short areas, water markets have emerged that also provide indications of marginal values. Evidence from these two sources suggests that (Brown 1999):

- Economic studies of water value tend to be performed, and water markets tend to develop,

where water is scarce. The values determined in such studies or markets are likely to overestimate values for water supplies where water is not so scarce.

- Marginal values of streamflow in any one use depend on the degree of water scarcity, which in turn depends on localized water demand and supply factors, including the capacities of water facilities like reservoirs and canals. Degree of scarcity is highly site-specific, which makes transferring values reliably from one site to another difficult.

- The marginal value of streamflow depends on the variety of uses to which the flow may be put. Its value for instream uses—producing electricity at hydroelectric plants or providing for habitat, recreation, and waste dilution—must be added to values in off-stream uses. Most diversions to off-stream uses consume some water but also provide some return flows that can be used by others downstream.

- The marginal value of streamflow in off-stream uses can be zero in locations with ample water supplies. Depending on recreation demand and hydroelectric plant capacities, the marginal value of water in instream uses may be positive even in water-rich areas.

- Although values vary widely from one site to another, for typical areas without ample water supply,

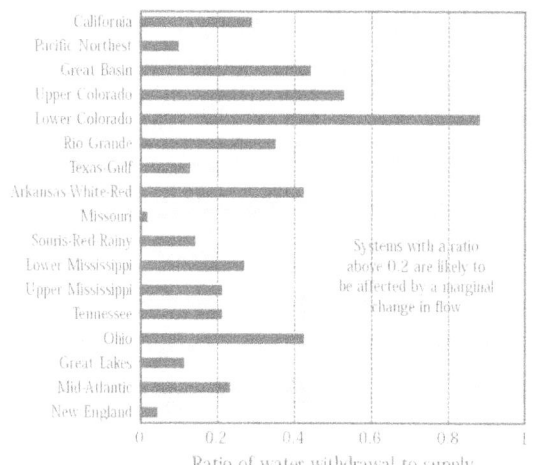

Figure 8. The proportion of water supply that is withdrawn to off-stream use in the 18 water-resource regions of the United States. If only a small proportion of available flow is diverted off-stream, off-stream users are unlikely to be affected by a small change in flow, except perhaps in very dry years. (Alaska and Hawaii not included)

economic studies and transaction evidence suggest a marginal value of streamflow delivered to off-stream uses of roughly $40 per acre-foot, on average. A few economic studies report higher values than this for municipal and industrial water, but the evidence is too limited to be applied to broad areas in large-scale assessments such as this one.

■ Marginal values of water in producing electricity at hydroelectric plants range as high as $40 per acre-foot for flow originating at the headwaters of one highly developed watershed, but the values are much lower for most places. Average values per acre-foot of flow in each of the 18 water-resource regions (U.S. Water Resources Council 1978) of the contiguous 48 States are conservatively estimated to range from $0.26 to $17.00, with most below $2.

■ Marginal values of streamflow for recreation differ widely from one site or season to another, depending on a host of factors, but evidence from economic studies suggests that the marginal value of streamflow for recreation is below $10 per acre-foot in most places.

■ The total value of streamflow from national forests depends on the average value over the entire amount of use, not on the marginal value. Because average values may greatly exceed marginal values, the average value of streamflow from national forests may be high even where the marginal value is modest, especially in watersheds where national forests contribute a substantial portion of the total water supply. Average values are not observed in the market place and are difficult to measure; therefore, estimating the total value of streamflow is difficult. Nevertheless, with appropriate assumptions and the use of marginal values as a lower bound on average values, a rough estimate of total value may be obtained.

■ The estimates of runoff from the national forests were adjusted to correct for discrepancies between the total land area within the mapped boundaries of the national forests and the area the Forest Service actually manages. As expected, the difference is greatest in Regions 8 and 9, where the Federal holdings are more fragmented. This correction removed the difference between the "gross acreage" and the "National Forest System acreage" (USDA Forest Service 1997). The volume of runoff from the national forests as estimated by the MAPSS model, corrected to reflect the actual land area under Forest Service management, is the national forest instream flow shown in column 2 of table 1.

Not all water is diverted for off-stream use and much water flows directly to the ocean without passing through irrigation canals, municipal diversions, or the like. Therefore, the numbers for water flowing from units of the National Forest System were corrected to include only the water actually used offstream. Data on water withdrawals were taken from the U.S. Geological Survey (Solley et al. 1998). The percentage of total runoff in each region attributable to national forest lands was divided by the total runoff from all lands in the corresponding Forest Service region, as determined by the MAPSS model. The resulting fraction was multiplied by the total runoff in each Forest Service region that goes to offstream uses based on the U.S. Geological Survey data. The results are shown in column 3 of table 1.

The lower bound on the value of runoff from Forest Service lands was estimated by applying the average marginal values discussed above (Brown 1999) to the estimates of water yield shown in table 1 for each Forest Service region. Withdrawals to offstream uses were valued at $40 per acre-foot, and instream flow was valued at $17 per acre-foot in the West and $8 per acre-foot in the East for recreation and hydropower combined. Dilution, navigation, and nonuse values were assumed to be nil. The results of these calculations are shown by Forest Service region in figure 9. The value of water flowing from national forests, in both offstream and instream uses, is conservatively estimated to be at least $3.7 billion per year.

This estimate makes it possible to compare the total value of the water originating on the national forests with similar values for other forest resources. It provides a general idea of the relative importance to

Table 1. Water Supply from National Forests by Forest Service Region

Sources: Derived from Solley et al. (1998) and Nelson (1995)

Region	National Forest Instream Flow	National Forest Offstream Use
	Acre-feet	*Acre-feet*
Northern	15,914,000	3,815,342
Rocky Mountain	9,144,792	2,150,811
Southwestern	7,428,051	1,971,245
Intermountain	11,458,855	4,785,689
Pacific Southwest	33,201,475	9,496,005
Pacific Northwest	44,658,346	4,806,316
Southern	19,041,809	3,587,515
Eastern	14,714,248	3,376,458

society of the various resources and equips the public to make informed decisions about alternative uses of their forests.

Water runoff is different from many other resources, in terms of the degree of Federal ownership and control. Although the agency generally has legal authority to decide about the sale or use of timber stumpage, livestock grazing, and recreation access, the Federal Government has not established a legal right to most of the water flowing from the forests. Hard-rock minerals and fish and wildlife present a contrasting case, more like that of water runoff. Locatable minerals are owned by the Federal Government, but the agency does not control access. Fish and wildlife are owned by the State, with access controlled by the agency and "take" controlled by the State. In both cases, although the resources are not owned by the Federal Government, they do have value to society, and in both cases the Forest Service estimates and reports on those values.

TRUE VALUE OF WATER IS UNDERESTIMATED

This estimate of of value understates the true value of water flowing from the national forests in three ways. First, our analysis counts marginal value rather than average value, even though average values may greatly exceed marginal values. Second, our estimates ignore values attached to navigation, waste dilution,

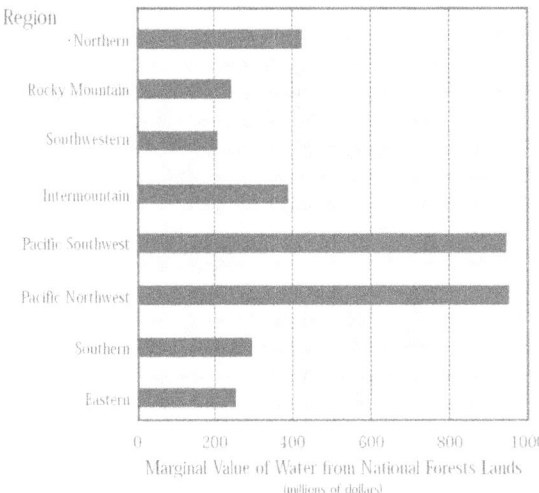

Figure 9. *Annual value of water from national forests by region. The marginal value of water from all national forest lands is at least $3.7 billion per year.*

channel maintenance, and such ecological services as aquatic habitats and wetland functions. Third, our analysis does not count nonuse values—existence value, option value, and bequest value—even though some studies indicate that nonuse values may be substantial. The values estimated through this analysis thus represent a lower limit on the range of values attributable to waters flowing from the national forests. The actual values of these flows are almost certainly higher, but how much higher is not known.

Providing cold, clear waters of high quality for aquatic organisms and human use is probably the proper focus for managing water on the National Forest System. There is relatively little management can do to increase total water yield. But forest management can have major effects on water quality—affecting temperature, nutrient loadings, sediment yields, and toxic contaminants. Management can also affect the storage capacity of soils and alluvial deposits, marginally affecting magnitude of peak streamflow and the duration of dry-season streamflows.

Water quality changes affect aquatic habitats, downstream water management facilities, recreation opportunities, and water treatment costs. Land management can cause increases in flood peaks and reduced channel stability, and impact the ability of downstream water users to benefit from the streamflow. The values of changes in the quality or timing of streamflows have received less attention by economists than has total quantity, partly because quality and timing are more difficult to monitor. The economic value of careful forest management—management that protects soils and water quality and takes full advantage of the watershed's ability to temporarily store water and ameliorate downstream flood damage—calls for additional study, but it is not addressed in detail in this paper. The economic analysis in this paper provides only a first approximation of the minimum value to society of the waters flowing from the national forests. Other measures of value attributable to national forest waters remain to be filled in by further studies

MANY COMMUNITIES DEPEND ON WATER FROM THE NATIONAL FORESTS

In 1999, the Environmental Protection Agency (EPA) estimated that 3,400 public drinking-water systems are located in watersheds containing national forest lands. About 60 million people live in these 3,400 communities. We will eventually have a more accurate picture of the role of the forests in providing municipal water supplies. All 50 States and many participating tribes are now delineating the surface watersheds and groundwater recharge areas that provide public drinking water to the 68,000 communities that rely on surface water or groundwater for their public water supplies. This effort will extend over the next 4 years, as required by the Safe Drinking Water Act.

In most of the West, a relatively few public water systems and watersheds supply most of the population. For example, in Washington State, 86 percent of the population is served by a few very large public water systems, nearly all of which draw from national forest lands. However, the 69 percent of public water systems that serve less than 100 connections (see figure 10) could also be of major concern to the Forest Service, because of the large number of such systems and the passion with which people pursue protection of their water supplies.

An update of the 1978 inventory by Region 6 showed that the number of communities in Oregon obtaining drinking water from National Forest System watersheds in 1998 was more than 50 percent higher than in 1978. Water from national forest lands supply about 80 percent of Oregon's population of 2.8 million people.

Figure 10. Washington's community water systems. A relatively small number of water systems supply large numbers of people. Numerous water systems serve small numbers of people each, but each of them that includes National Forest could be an important issue for the Forest Service.

The Siuslaw National Forest in Region 6 has identified 136 public water systems on national forest lands encompassing 36 percent of the forest. Municipal water supply watersheds encompass 85 percent of the Rogue River National Forest and 94 percent of the Umpqua National Forest.

In the Northern United States (21 States), 76.5 million people are served by water from nearly 4,000 surface water systems. National forest lands contain 925 water systems serving about 7.75 million people. In Massachusetts, 11 percent of the area of the State serves the water needs of nearly 7 million people. The municipal watersheds there are more than 72 percent forested. New York City's municipal watershed is more than 60 percent actively managed forest.

California's State Water Project, with 22 dams and 600 miles of canals, delivers water that originates largely on national forest lands in the Sierra Nevada—more than 2 million acre-feet annually—to 20 million urban and agricultural users in both the San Francisco Bay and southern California. The Federal Central Valley Project includes another 20 reservoirs and more than 500 miles of canals that deliver another 7 million acre-feet to irrigate 3 million acres in the Central Valley and provide drinking water to 2 million urbanites.

More than 900 cities rely on National Forest System watersheds, including: Portland, Salem, Eugene, and Medford, OR; Eureka, Oakland, and Berkeley, CA; Denver, Fort Collins, and Colorado Springs, CO; Hele-

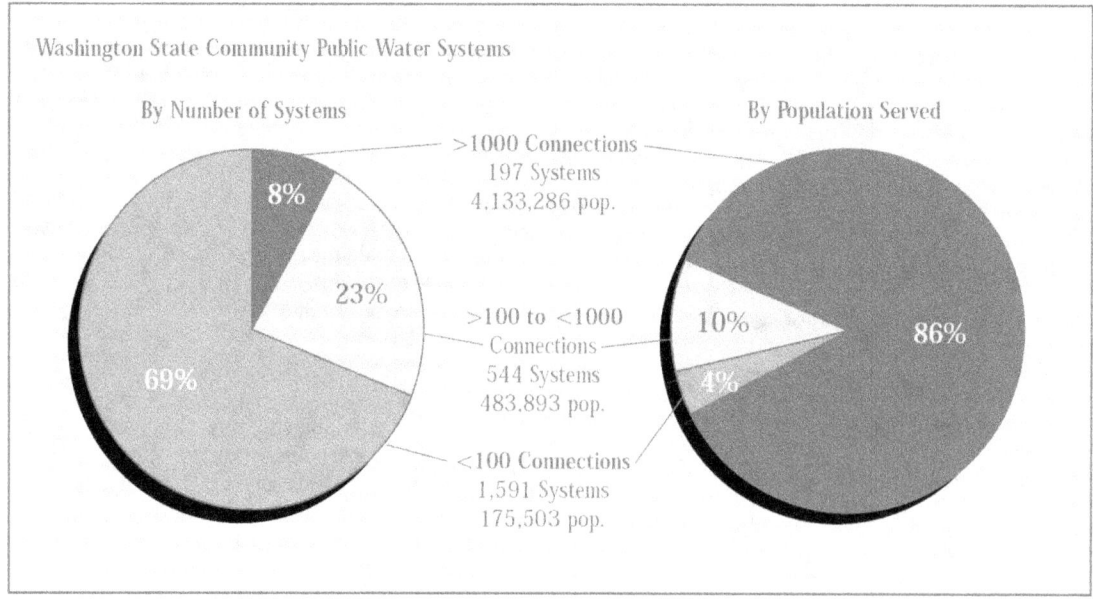

Washington State Community Public Water Systems

By Number of Systems

By Population Served

>1000 Connections
197 Systems
4,133,286 pop.

8%

23%

69%

>100 to <1000
Connections
544 Systems
483,893 pop.

<100 Connections
1,591 Systems
175,503 pop.

10%

4%

86%

na, Butte, and Bozeman, MT; Salt Lake City, UT; Reno, and Carson City, NV; Little Rock, AR; and Ely, MN. Relatively more western than eastern cities use national forest water because of the relatively larger land base in the Western States.

Should municipal watersheds be managed under an active or a passive regime? Many Forest Service specialists believe that long-term supplies of high-quality water can best be sustained under an active program of vegetation management designed to maintain the forest system and watershed processes within their natural range of variability. Many people in urban centers believe that humans should not alter watersheds in any way, other than to divert water. The scientific evidence indicates that watersheds can be effectively managed for high-quality water while providing for other resource outputs as byproducts. ❖

Water Quantity Issues for Forest Planning

STREAMFLOW REGIMES, TIMING, AND FLOODS

The experience of widespread flooding and sedimentation following on the heels of logging and fire was one of the primary reasons for establishing national forests. The timing of water yields was also an important issue, especially the desire to augment late-season flows. Extending the irrigation season and limiting the adverse effects of drought were also significant concerns.

A wide range of human activities, including forest management, roads, reservoir and dam operation, loss of wetlands, development and urbanization of floodplains and other flood-prone areas, and stream channelizing have been implicated as factors increasing the destructive potential of floods.

A wide range of agencies is responsible for various aspects of flood prediction and control, but no one agency or group of agencies is charged with evaluating the consequences of its actions in relationship to other parties. Although forest practices may increase peak flows and sediment transport from upland streams, downstream effects may be minimized where reservoir operation reduces flood peaks and sediment accumulates in reservoirs. On the other hand, sustained high-flow releases from dams may contribute to higher sediment and turbidity problems downstream compared to shorter but higher natural peak flows.

In the Intermountain and Southwest Regions, the relationship between healthy vegetation groundcover and reduction of summer floods from high-intensity storms has been well established, as summarized by Coleman (1953) (see figure 11).

The change in runoff associated with different degrees of ground cover shows that watershed cover and on-site water control measures can reduce flood threats. Similar reductions in flood peaks have been observed in the East after watershed restoration. For more humid areas, the effect of vegetation management and healthy upland watershed conditions is still important in limiting erosion and sedimentation effects from floods.

Substantial and dependable beneficial shifts in timing of peak runoff are unlikely to be achieved through managing forest vegetation and snow. In the Eastern United States and to some degree in the West, harvest

Figure 11. Experimental results of the effects of watershed condition on rainstorm runoff and erosion (data from Great Basin Experimental Area, UT).

GOOD Ground Cover
60-75% of ground covered
with plants and litter

Surface
Runoff
2% of rainfall

Soil Loss
0.05 Tons
per acre

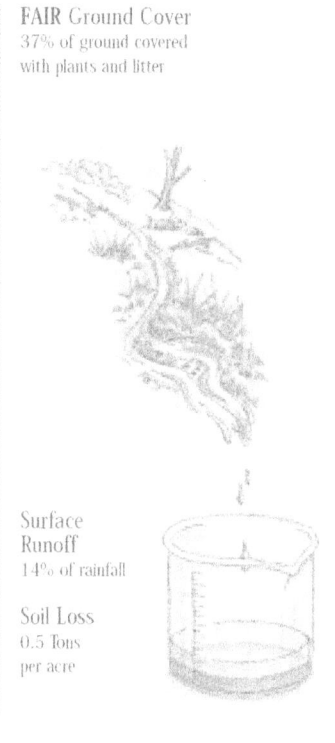

FAIR Ground Cover
37% of ground covered
with plants and litter

Surface
Runoff
14% of rainfall

Soil Loss
0.5 Tons
per acre

POOR Ground Cover
10% of ground covered
with plants and litter

Surface
Runoff
73% of rainfall

Soil Loss
5.55 Tons
per acre

activities have increased late-season flows. These changes are typically short lived, however, because of vegetation regrowth. Sustaining late-season flows is an important issue and limited scientific studies have focused on the relation between healthy watershed conditions and sustaining late-summer flows. Anecdotal observations from a variety of watershed and channel restoration projects suggest that perennial flows have often been restored to apparently ephemeral channels by managing and restoring vegetation. Many watersheds and meadows have been incised as a result of poorly located travelways and roads. Other areas have greatly expanded channel networks as a result of excessive livestock use that produced gullys and incised channels. The effect of these slope, meadow, and channel incisions is to drain local groundwater storage and transmit flows downstream more rapidly. This process leaves little effective ground storage to sustain late-season flows or to carry over water storage into a drought year. Preventing incisions and restoring incised slopes, meadows, and streams could improve late-season flows (see figure 12). Improving these conditions should be a focus of watershed restoration efforts. Concurrently, additional research is needed to understand the process and consequences of incision and the values obtained in late season flows through restoration activities. Roads and their effects on draining slopes and increasing channel density need additional study as well.

In summary, limited but valuable opportunities through forest management could shift the timing of flows. A vital aspect is to prevent or limit incisions in slopes, meadows, and channels. Treatments that restore these areas and thus restore the relation of channels to the floodplains and increase the contact time of runoff on slopes and meadows are likely to recharge soil profiles and shallow ground water reservoirs, which would greatly increase the likelihood of sustaining late-season flows.

AUGMENTING STREAMFLOW

Producing substantial and extensive increases in water yields from the national forests does not appear to be practical. Research has demonstrated that water yields can be increased by removing vegetation and trapping additional snow. But application of the vegetation management practices needed to increase flows on a watershed scale is limited in practice by Forest Service mandates to manage for a wide range of resource values. Legal constraints, land allocations, technological limits, as well as societal values and environmental, ecological, and biological concerns all favor not committing national forest lands to the management regimes that would be needed to increase water yields.

Ziemer (1987) offers one of the best summaries and evaluations of the potentials and limitations of augmenting water yield on forested lands in the United States. His findings indicated that for a variety of reasons, water yield increases are likely to be undetectable. Forest research has demonstrated that cutting trees, type converting of brush to grass, and snow management can produce increased water yields. These increases generally come from lands that receive more than 15 inches of annual precipitation. In general, areas with higher precipitation, typified by mixed conifer species; spruce, fir, and lodgepole pine forests; and eastern hardwoods produce more yield per unit area than other forest types.

Although water-yield increases can result from forest management activities, the increases produced by normal silvicultural methods applied in the context of multiple use are modest. Even in wet environments of the Northwest (Harr 1983) and the Sierra Nevada of California (Kattelmann and others 1983) these

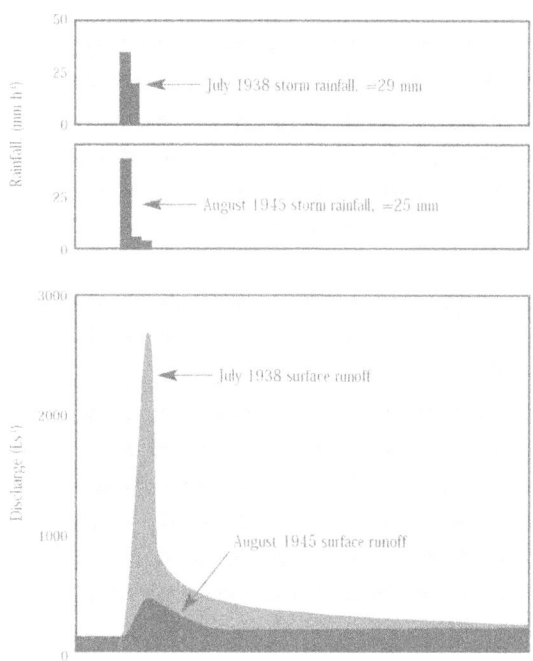

Figure 12. Comparative rainfall and storm runoff hydrographs, White Hollow, TN, before and after watershed rehabilitation.

increases could be in the range of 6 percent, if water yield were strongly emphasized, but more likely 1 percent under normal management. Detecting and measuring this small change is outside the limits of current technology (Ziemer 1987). The most productive areas for this potential would have the shortest duration because of rapid regrowth of vegetation reoccupying the site.

Properly evaluating augmentation potential often overlooks the legacy of historical forest management actions. Frequently, much of the potential for augmentation is already being realized. For example, in the Southwest, Schmidt and Solomon (1981) estimated that about 50 percent of the potential was already being realized.

Strategies for dealing with water shortages should avoid relying on augmentation from national forests as a substitute for practices to reduce water consumption and improve conservation.

INSTREAM FLOW REQUIREMENTS

Sustaining viable native populations of aquatic species on national forest lands will require securing instream flows that fall within the range of natural variation. Natural streamflows exhibit complex regimes, with important and life-sustaining variations in their frequency, magnitude, duration, and timing. Fish and other aquatic and riparian organisms depend directly on this regime and the habitats that it forms and maintains. Some departure from these regimes is tolerable and will not extirpate organisms, but this threshold is difficult to define. The Forest Service must actively participate in the processes that allocate water and water rights to secure instream flows sufficient to sustain native populations.

Policy Implications

Forest plans should be integrated with watershed assessments (assessments are conducted on all lands within a watershed not just national forest lands) and with watershed recovery plans so that goals are clear and of sufficient scope to include watershed management and restoration opportunities across ownerships. See figure 13 for examples of past and future strategies to obtain instream flows.

Greater involvement of partners and other members of the public in the planning process would likely need a better understanding of the need to integrate management opportunities on all lands within a watershed including private lands.

Forest plans, when they are revised, should identify

and quantify the amounts of surface and groundwater needed to meet present and future consumptive and instream water uses on national forest lands. When a State undertakes a basinwide adjudication of water rights, all beneficial water uses on national forest lands should be claimed in accordance with Federal and State procedural and substantive laws and regulations, unless otherwise directed by the Office of the General Counsel. Forest planning should use the most defensible methods and avoid inconsistent and piecemeal analyses.

Early and intensive collaboration among existing and potential water users is a cost-efficient approach in most situations. Public collaboration in forest planning can achieve acceptable solutions and may lessen or avoid the costly litigation common to water rights issues.

In many places, the Forest Service lacks the necessary technical expertise in hydrology. Our present level of in-house expertise must be conserved and

Figures 13. Past strategies have been to litigate to secure favorable flows and protect the public interest. In the future, the agency will incorporate flows needed to meet multiple-use mandates through forest planning, as well as by litigation and negotiation.

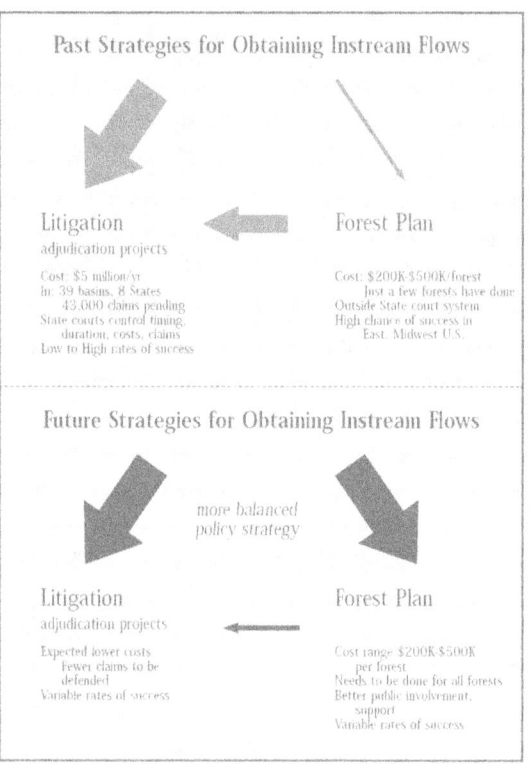

enhanced if costly failures, both in collaboration and in court, are to be avoided.

FERC RELICENSING

From the 1940's to the 1960's, 325 hydroelectric projects were licensed and built on the national forests (see table 2). These facilities have generated power and provided recreation opportunities. But building and operating these projects has also resulted in significant adverse effects on national forest resources. During the next 10 years, as more than 180 of these projects come up for relicensing, the Forest Service will have a unique opportunity to determine how these projects will operate for the next 30 to 50 years. The relicensing process presents the only chance for the Forest Service to reverse existing resource damage, improve water quality and aquatic habitat, mitigate future adverse effects, and significantly increase recreational opportunities to forest users.

The national distribution of dams provides an interesting look at how these dams are spread across national forest lands (see figures 14 and 15).

Table 2. Hydroelectric dams licensed by the FERC in each Forests Service region, both on and off national forests lands. Data derived from the National Inventory of Dams maintained by the U.S. Army Corps of Engineers, compiled and developed by the Pacific Northwest Research Station.

Forest Service Region	Number on NFS land	Number off NFS land	Total
Northern (R1)	9	21	30
Rocky Mountain (R2)	21	71	92
Southwest (R3)	3	3	6
Intermountain (R4)	10	34	44
Pacific Southwest (R5)	152	87	239
Pacific Northwest (R6)	35	74	109
Southern (R8)	49	246	295
Eastern (R9)	31	1,318	1,349
Alaska (R10)	15	15	30
Total	325	1,869	2,194

Figure 14. Hydroelectric dams in the 48 States both on and off national forest lands. The largest number of small hydroelectric dams is in the New England, Great Lakes, southern Appalachian, and Mid Atlantic areas.

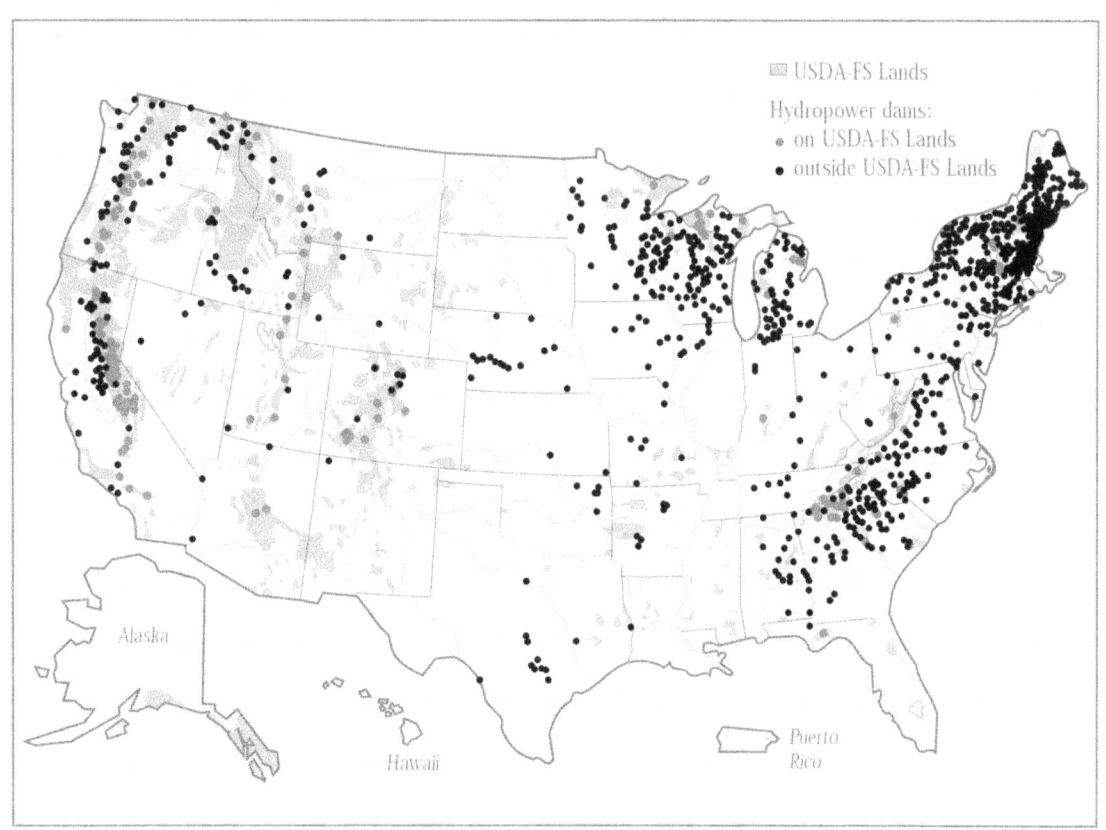

USDA-FS Lands

Hydropower dams:
- on USDA-FS Lands
- outside USDA-FS Lands

Alaska

Hawaii

Puerto Rico

There are nearly 2,200 hydroelectric dams in the United States, excluding Hawaii and Puerto Rico; about 15 percent of these are on national forest lands. Forest Service strategies for dealing with relicensing may differ among the regions because the issues and complexity vary with factors such as dam size, the river basin and biological contexts, interbasin water transfers, and cumulative effects.

The large-scale hydrologic effects of American dams have recently been assessed by Graf (1999). Graf found that the greatest density of dams and the greatest segmentation of river systems in California, the Texas-Gulf, and South Atlantic water resource regions (see figures 14 and 15). Regions with high ratios of storage capacity to drainage area show the highest potential for changes to instream flows and ecological disruption. The greatest flow effects are in some western mountain and plain regions, where dams can store more than 3 years of runoff. The least effects to flow are in the Northeast, Upper Midwest, and Northwest where storage is as little as 25 percent of the annual runoff.

The regional variability of impacts and numbers of dams suggests that the Forest Service cannot tackle every dam relicensing on national forests with the same intensity. Nationally and regionally, we must focus strategically on the basins and dams where we can expect to achieve the greatest benefits for biodiversity, recreation, and ecosystem function in large, complex, mixed-ownership watersheds.

The Forest Service has binding statutory authority and responsibility from the Federal Power Act (FPA) to stipulate license conditions the Federal Energy Regulatory Commission (FERC) must include in the new license. To successfully condition these licenses, the Forest Service must develop a substantial and defensible administrative record to support the articles that have been "demonstrated necessary for the adequate protection and utilization of national forest resources." Developing the administrative record requires a significant commitment by the Forest Ser-

Figure 15. Hydroelectric dams in the 48 States on national forest lands. The largest number of these dams are on the west coast.

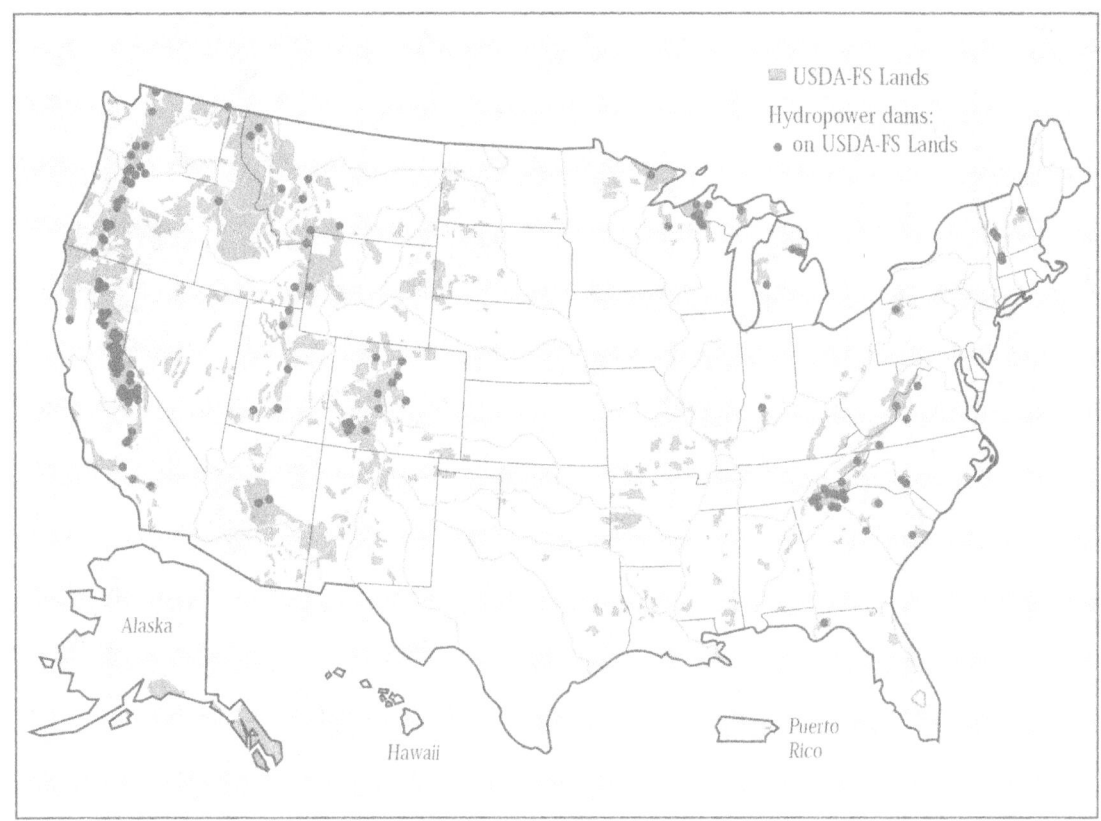

vice in terms of technical and process personnel and financial support. Relicensing processes normally take 5 to 10 years.

Forest Service participation in the relicensing process could strengthen mitigation and restoration programs on national forest lands that would lead to improved aquatic habitats and increased water quality. Estimates of these benefits to national forest lands exceed a billion dollars. Recreation, fish and wildlife, and watershed resources are the primary areas affected by hydroelectric generation, and these resources stand to realize the greatest benefits from the relicensing efforts. Potential benefits include new and upgraded recreational facilities, restored instream flow regimes, enhanced aquatic habitats, and improved wildlife habitat. Recent relicensing experiences have demonstrated that the benefit-to-cost ratio can be greater than 30:1; no other Forest Service program has a higher potential payoff.

GROUNDWATER

The groundwater resource under the surface of national forest lands has never been assessed at the national, regional, or forest scales. The U.S. Geological Survey has compiled a national atlas of groundwater in the United States, and published detailed regional studies of all major aquifers. Although neither of these sources show national forest lands, we can infer some things from them about groundwater in some parts of the national forest lands. We also have access to well logs where wells have been drilled on national forest lands by the agency or others. Many forest acres serve as recharge areas for aquifers in nearby valleys that many citizens depend on for their drinking and irrigation water. We are unable to quantify the amount, timing, or quality of this recharge with available data.

Over centuries, groundwater has been replenished by inflows from rivers, lakes, and wetlands. At shallow depths, the water table fluctuates with annual precipitation affecting lake levels and river flows. The value of groundwater depends on the depth of the water table due to drilling and pumping costs. We are not aware of any studies that have quantified the economic values of groundwater functions.

The States vary in their regulation of underground water. In many States, there is little if any regulation or monitoring of the extraction of underground water and there are unresolved jurisdictional questions over who has control over water extraction within the boundaries of the forests.

The ownership of groundwater is unresolved or unaddressed in many States. For example, the State of Virginia claims the water underlying Federal lands and it remains unclear if such a claim has merit.

Some existing special use permits involve the extraction of groundwater on national forest lands, but there is no agency policy on environmental effect analysis, valuation, metering, or resale of this water.

At least three groundwater-related issues affect national forest lands:

- Some communities want to change from contaminated groundwater wells to surface water supplies, and national forests are the logical or sole source.
- Groundwater extraction by adjacent communities or landowners may be drying up nearby streams and affecting riparian vegetation and aquatic habitat.
- The status of groundwater ownership within the national forests is unresolved in many States. The Forest Service lacks the scientific expertise and data on the groundwater resources underlying its lands to effectively cope with these growing issues.

Policy Implications

The growth of urban interface adjacent to the National Forest System has exceeded the agency's ability to respond to the challenges of increased water demand. Most current forest plans do not address water resources in a comprehensive manner. Forests are not adequately staffed with technical experts to handle the issues related to water that evolve faster than they can be inventoried. Claims on water originating from the National Forest System far outstrip the agency's ability to track them, much less manage the issues.

Starting points for developing an effective approach to the complex issues involved in water resources management include: a comprehensive inventory of State law, an analysis of conflicts with agency resource management objectives, and a complete inventory of Water Rights that are vested in the United States (within the National Forest System). ❖

Water Quality

Forested watersheds have a well-deserved reputation for producing clean water. The Forest Service has conducted long-term research on the effects of land management on water quality at experimental forests—such as Hubbard Brook in New Hampshire, H. J. Andrews in Oregon, and Coweeta in North Carolina. Research shows that the quality of water in undisturbed forests and grasslands is usually good. In managed ecosystems, water quality depends on the particular land-use practices being implemented. Some land-use practices can protect or restore water quality, but others may degrade or pose risks to clean water. Long-term studies conducted by the Forest Service have provided much of the current understanding of watershed processes in forests and grasslands, and such studies will need to be continued to assess the effects of forest management on water quality at landscape scales and over longer periods of time.

Most watersheds have several different land uses that affect source waters in complex patterns. These uses overlap across the landscape and change over time. A few studies have examined the interactions among multiple land uses and their cumulative effects over time, but most have examined small watersheds over short periods. More information is needed to assist managers in dealing with the complexity of these interactions for larger watersheds and longer time periods.

A key action of the Clean Water Action Plan directs the Departments of Agriculture and the Interior to consult with other Federal agencies, States, tribes, and other stakeholders to develop a Unified Federal Policy to enhance watershed management for protecting water quality and the health of aquatic ecosystems on Federal lands. The purpose of the Unified Federal Policy is to ensure a consistent approach to managing Federal lands on a watershed basis, to protect, maintain, and improve watershed conditions and water quality.

In summary, forests and grasslands often produce high-quality water. Long- term studies have shown this to be generally true in undisturbed ecosystems and for some classes of land use. Other forms of land use have been found to degrade water quality to varying degrees. The most significant water quality problems found on national forests are typically sediment (turbidity and bedload), nutrients, temperature, and hazardous chemicals. Measures to protect, restore, or mitigate water quality have been devised for many management practices. New research will be needed to understand the effects on water quality of innovative land management systems currently being devised as part of ecosystem management and to understand the cumulative effects of multiple management actions that overlap in space and time across large landscapes.

TOTAL MAXIMUM DAILY LOADS

Section 303(d) of the Clean Water Act requires that total maximum daily loads (TMDL) be established by States, tribes, U.S. territories, and EPA for waterbodies for which water quality standards are not being attained. Such waterbodies are generally referred to as "impaired" or "water quality limited." Forest Service policy is to participate in preparing and implementing TMDL's. The Forest Service is collaborating with the EPA and Bureau of Land Management (BLM) to prepare a policy and framework for developing and implementing TMDL's in forest and rangeland environments.

TMDL's for a pollutant is defined by the EPA as the sum of the waste load allocation for point sources, plus load allocation for nonpoint sources of pollution, plus a load to allow a margin of safety (40 CFR 130.2). The load allocation for nonpoint sources of pollution includes "natural" background loads and the margin of safety accounts for uncertainty. The TMDL approach is a mechanism for improving impaired waters and a process for determining tradeoffs between point and nonpoint sources. It provides a focus for future watershed management actions.

A collaborative approach by all landowners in a watershed is the potential strength of the TMDL process. Its weaknesses are the current technical and scientific barriers to connecting water-quality standards to specific nonpoint sources, particularly where the pollutants of concern are native components of stream systems, like sediment and heat. Because of highly variable natural background regimes and long delays between the introduction of pollutants and downstream effects, relating water quality standards to the effectiveness of individual control measures is often difficult or impossible. The lack of precision and reliability limits the utility of the TMDL process in allocating loads to specific management practices or to individual landowners in forest and rangeland settings. Creative approaches will be needed to salvage useful gains from a legal framework that was designed for point-source pollution control and fits nonpoint source control poorly. The Forest Service should continue to develop and monitor best management practices, ensure a high rate of implementation, and revise those practices that are not effective, as the fundamental basis of our water quality management program.

New technology developed by EPA and the Forest Service for temperature monitoring uses forward-looking infrared radar to provide a spatially continuous thermal profile over hundreds of miles of streams. This technology is providing a framework for restoring water quality and a picture of what sections are meeting and not meeting water-quality standards for temperature. This relatively cheap and accurate method is an important tool in providing landscape context to water-quality problems.

ABANDONED MINE LANDS AND HAZARDOUS MATERIALS SITES

At least 38,000 abandoned mine lands and hazardous material waste sites exist on national forest lands. These sites, most common on western forests, often cause severe and chronic water pollution. In the early 1990's EPA proposed that discharges from abandoned mines be subject to permits under the Clean Water Act. As an alternative, a "watershed approach" agreement was made to coordinate the efforts of all land managers and owners to efficiently and comprehensively address restoration projects in entire watersheds, rather than spot-treating individual sites. Key steps in the interagency agreement include setting priorities—among watersheds in each State and mine sites within each priority watershed—and monitoring. Several watersheds were selected as pilots, including Boulder River in Montana and Upper Animas River in Colorado. Now included in the Clean Water Action Plan, cooperation and collaboration among States, Federal agencies, and tribes is fundamental to the watershed approach. This program is relatively new, and few mines have been completely restored. ❖

Watershed Condition and Restoration

ational forest activities have affected water quality and productivity of the land. Problem watersheds and processes are often masked by the size of the landscape, or noticeable only when flooding or other disturbances occur. Although most watersheds on national forests appear healthy on a large scale, extensive localized rehabilitation needs still exist on these lands.

Concerns include soil degradation, lack of vegetative cover, eroding stream channels, gullies, landslides, abandoned roads, and compacted rangeland. Some watersheds can be restored by emphasizing land management requirements and practices. Some watersheds are so seriously affected that making a difference will be hard. Other watersheds are expected to respond to intensive investment in erosion control features. Some types of work are intensive, structural, and expensive for a relatively small site and need to be monitored and maintained. Biological treatments, like seeding, are extensive and require little maintenance.

Disturbances in forest and grassland vegetation from drought, wind, fire, insects, and diseases are part of properly functioning ecosystems in watersheds. However, some past management practices—such as fire exclusion, timber harvesting, and human development—have created watersheds that experience more frequent or intense fire disturbances than in the past. Many of these forests and grasslands are overcrowded with increased susceptibility to drought, and insect and disease outbreaks. The excessive amounts of dead wood and grass, especially in watersheds that historically burned at frequent intervals, heighten the risk of high-intensity, destructive fires. Large-scale vegetative disturbances in a watershed adversely affect waterbodies by increasing soil erosion and nutrient runoff. With dense stands of vegetation and large amounts of dead fuel on the ground, the size and intensity of fires can increase significantly and be accompanied by greater risks of erosion, severity of floods, and decreases in water quality.

The long-term view is that healthy watersheds can only be achieved if the ecosystems on the watershed are healthy. Watershed restoration includes recovery of natural timber and grass stands and fuels composition. Thinning, prescribed burning, and other management projects are needed on a watershed (landscape) scale to significantly alter the predicted course of events leading toward large-scale erosion, flooding, and nutrient loss on disturbed watersheds.

In the most comprehensive landscape assessment to date—the Interior Columbia Basin Assessment—current condition of forest and rangeland areas had drastically departed from the historical condition. Fire suppression and harvest of the large pine trees resulted in the buildup of fuels and changes in the ponderosa pine forests. Rangelands have been invaded by exotic weeds. Different management scenarios were modeled out over the next 100 years.

The model found that, at the landscape scale, current momentum toward further departure from the desired condition will not be overcome in the next 100 years, even with the most aggressive proposed management. Management could not reverse the trend of forest changes at current or reasonably foreseeable levels of staff, activities, and budget.

The sobering news is that, in the Interior Columbia Basin, forest and range health restoration will proceed at such a slow rate that unnaturally large, high-intensity fires will continue to reset landscape vegetation. This is probably true in many other areas as well. These findings suggest that a more realistic assessment of the prospects for success is needed; effective restoration of all degraded areas is simply not feasible. We do not have the resources to make a difference at landscape scale unless we strategically focus our restoration efforts. Focusing on selected watersheds at the scale of 200,000 to 500,000 acres, where we can hope to make a difference, is a more realistic and promising approach.

WETLANDS AND RIPARIAN AREAS

Of the nearly 192 million acres managed as national forests and grasslands, fewer than 10 percent are considered wetlands and riparian areas. Higher percentages are found in Regions 8, 9, and 10 with significantly lower percentages (less than 2 percent) in the arid and semi-arid portions of Regions 1, 2, 3, 4, 5, and 6. These are rough estimates because the Forest Service has not conducted specific inventories of these areas. Because of their limited extent and usually narrow configuration, wetlands and riparian areas have often been mapped as inclusions in larger mapping units during soil surveys, range analysis, and other inventory and analysis efforts. A more definitive estimate is needed for improved management.

These areas are often the most productive and most used portions of the landscape because they have more available water, deeper and more fertile soils, robust vegetation, and cooling shade. Riparian and wetland areas also receive the most intense use because they provide abundant forage for wildlife and domestic livestock, serve as transportation corridors, commonly produce quality timber, concentrate recreational use, and may hold valued minerals.

The total grazing use of Federal lands has decreased steadily since the mid-1950's. However, in the Pacific Northwest, grazing has increased on private lands near waterbodies and in riparian areas, bringing corresponding increases in grazing-related damage to riparian function and watershed condition.

The condition of riparian areas and wetlands varies considerably across the Nation, depending on a number of physical and land use factors. Estimates indicate that conditions on national forest lands are good in over 90 percent of Alaska, 70 percent of the East, 60 percent of the South, and in the West ranges from over 50 percent in the more humid sections to less than 30 percent in semiarid and arid areas. Reasons for poor conditions vary significantly across the country. Past timber harvest, roading, recreation, and urban encroachment account for much of the problems in the East, South, Alaska, and humid portions of the West. Livestock grazing, roading, recreation, mining, and urban encroachment account for much of the concern in the drier parts of the West.

Although these areas are easily overused and damaged, they also respond quickly to improved management. Watershed improvement programs, fisheries habitat improvements, range betterment efforts, enlightened road placement and maintenance, and restoration of abandoned mines all contribute to improving these important areas. Key elements of the Forest Service's Natural Resources Agenda and Clean Water Action Plan focus on restoring and managing wetland and riparian areas.

Roads

After the Second World War, the growing demand for wood products fueled an exponential growth in forest road mileage. From a limited mileage in 1960, the system of forest roads has grown to more than 400,000 miles. During this period, conventional wisdom held that as long as a road remained intact—comfortably drivable—the surrounding area would benefit from increased access. People also believed that adverse effects from roads could be corrected and that physical and biological resources would not suffer long-term changes. The engineering emphasis was on protecting the road from damage by water; other physical or biological effects received little attention. In fact, many roads posed severe problems and risks for forest resources, both as land disturbance and as

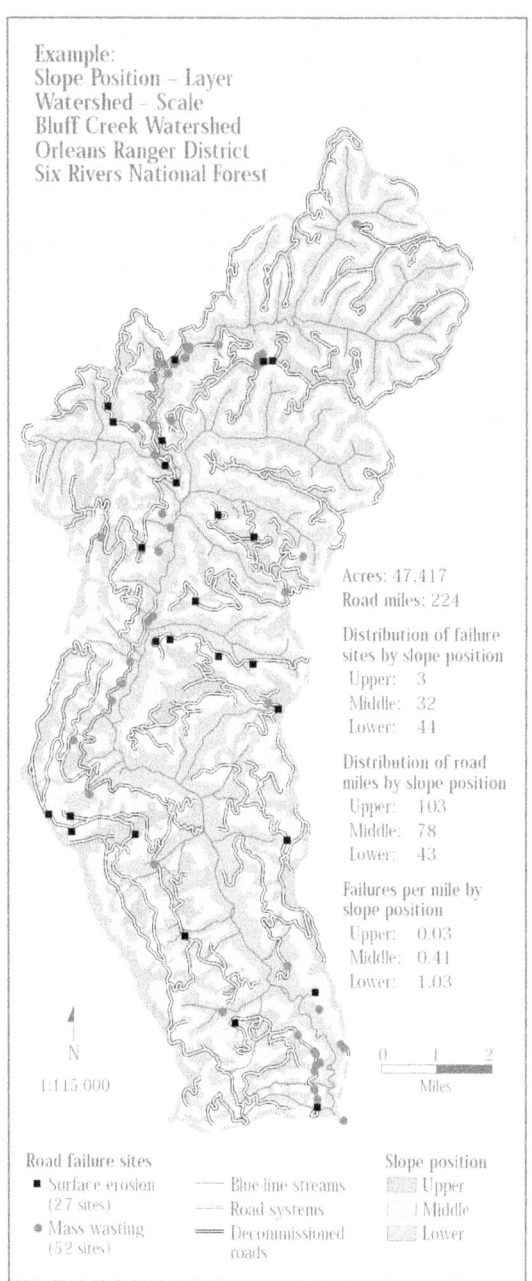

Figure 16. Road failures are strongly related to slope position in this northern California watershed. Note that most of the failures are in middle and lower positions, with only three in the upper slope position (USDA Forest Service 1999). Effects vary greatly among roads, and substantial effort is needed to distinguish high-impact and low-impact roads to set priorities for watershed restoration.

Example:
Slope Position – Layer
Watershed – Scale
Bluff Creek Watershed
Orleans Ranger District
Six Rivers National Forest

Acres: 47,417
Road miles: 224

Distribution of failure
sites by slope position
Upper: 3
Middle: 32
Lower: 44

Distribution of road
miles by slope position
Upper: 103
Middle: 78
Lower: 43

Failures per mile by
slope position
Upper: 0.03
Middle: 0.41
Lower: 1.03

N
1:115,000

0   1   2
Miles

Road failure sites
■ Surface erosion
   (27 sites)
● Mass wasting
   (52 sites)

—— Blue-line streams
---- Road systems
══ Decommissioned
     roads

Slope position
▨ Upper
▧ Middle
▨ Lower

access routes that concentrate human activities and pollution. Damages to watersheds and aquatic and riparian ecosystems accumulated in many places.

In recent years, a growing concern for water quality, runoff, and flood damage in forests and rangelands has focused attention on roads and their effects on water quality and watershed functions. The current Forest Service Natural Resources Agenda reflects this concern.

Many studies have shown that roads in forests have elevated erosion rates and often increase the likelihood of landslides in steep or unstable terrain. Both of these effects can be especially pronounced where roads cross or run near streams, resulting in sediment discharge to surface waters. Roads are also likely sites for chemical spills associated with traffic accidents, with the highest risk of water contamination where roads cross streams. Proper road engineering, application of Best Management Practices (BMP), and emergency preparedness can reduce but not eliminate these risks. Unfortunately, most of the roads on national forests and grasslands were built before current engineering practices and BMP's were used, and the cost of upgrading to current standards is high.

Other transportation corridors, such as pipelines and powerline rights-of-way, also pose problems and risks.

Not all roads have the same effects on watersheds. Variation is great and discriminating between high-impact and low-impact roads and road networks is an important analytical challenge. For example, studies on national forest watersheds in northern California (USDA 1999) found that roads at or near ridgetops had far fewer failures and generated far less sediment to streams than roads in lower slope positions (see figure 16) . The specific effects of roads are strongly influenced by a variety of factors, including road building techniques, soils and bedrock, topography, and severity of storm events.

Research has shown that improved design, construction, and maintenance can reduce the effects of roads on water quality, wetlands, and watershed function. Remarkably little is known about road effects on hydrology at watershed and subbasin scales, so there is inadequate basis to evaluate the hydrologic functioning of the road system at large scales. Analytical techniques need to be developed further. The specific range of ongoing and likely watershed effects should be evaluated at both regional and landscape scales. ❖

Conserving Aquatic Biodiversity and Threatened Species

/ In conserving and recovering at-risk species and maintaining biodiversity, a strong consensus among conservation biologists supports the need for refugia or designated areas capable of providing high-quality habitat. For aquatic species, watersheds are the basic unit for such a conservation strategy. Watersheds that have maintained hydrologic functions and processes, and those that support healthy populations of the species of interest or their specific habitats have been identified. These areas receive a combination of low-risk land allocations, special land-use standards, or priority for analysis and restoration efforts.

Networks of refugia must be large and well distributed to anchor the persistence and recovery of the at-risk species in current and future disturbance regimes and ever-changing landforms and vegetation cover. Refugia alone are not assumed to be sufficient to conserve species. Lands between refugia are expected to be subject to land allocations and practices that will promote watershed function and conserve species, complementing the special focus on refugia.

Some aquatic species (for example, invertebrates) depend on local habitats. They may exist only in a single spring or a spring-stream system in a single watershed. Where habitats are isolated or unique (because of water chemistry, vegetation, and a multitude of contributing factors), the potential for rare species is high. The distribution of these habitats is not restricted to any set of watersheds, lithology, or other ecological units. The importance of these "rare" habitats must be recognized, with proper inventory and site-specific protection measures.

Where lands are set aside or allocated for special low-risk management, broad conservation benefits accrue, not just for targeted rare species, but for biodiversity and watershed health as well. These areas provide a hedge against unanticipated problems with species viability and large-scale disturbances and climate changes.

Five recent, large-scale, ecosystem-based Forest Service assessments have identified networks of aquatic conservation watersheds: the Northwest Forest Plan (FEMAT 1993), the Interior Columbia Basin Ecosystem Management Project, The Tongass National Forest Land Management Plan, the Sierra Nevada Framework Project, and the Southern Appalachians Assessment.

Of these, the Northwest Forest Plan and the Tongass National Forest Land Management Plan have records of decision that delineate key watersheds or central areas for biodiversity. The stage is set and progress is being made in the other areas to identify special emphasis watersheds and to protect and, where needed, restore them.

Table 3. Land areas identified for aquatic conservation, biodiversity, and clean water in various recent large-scale ecosystem analyses.

Assessement Area	Number of Refugia watersheds	Total area, refugia watersheds (acres)	Proportion of total NF area*
Northwest Forest Plan (key watersheds) [1]	164	8,678,600 (includes BLM lands)	33%
Tongass National Forest [2]	Too many to count	13,662,000**	80%
Interior Columbia Basin (strongholds) [3]	1,693	19,977,824 (includes BLM)	40%
Sierra Nevada [4] (proposed emphasis watersheds)	139	5,747,261	47%
Southern Appalachians (aquatic diversity areas) [5]	45	10,303,360 (17% is National Forest)	38%

*In the analysis area.
** Conserve and restore land use designations
1. FEMAT 1994.
2. Tongass Land Management Plan revision, 1997.
3. Interior Columbia Basin Ecosystem Management Project.
4. Draft information from of the Sierra Framework project, Pacific Southwest Region (Joseph Furnish, pers. comm).
5. Southern Appalachian Assessment.

Conserving Aquatic Biodiversity and Threatened Species

These efforts represent a substantial actual and potential commitment of lands to conserving aquatic species and could be regarded as a major part of a national forest aquatic and biodiversity conservation strategy. More than 53 percent of national forest lands are represented by the assessments in table 3. The role that the national forest lands play in anchoring fish and other aquatic species is not trivial, with greater than one-third of national forest lands identified as important to maintaining aquatic biodiversity.

The Inland West Water Initiative, which includes Regions 1, 2, 3, and 4, will have completed its assessment and delineated special waterbodies and watersheds by early FY 2000. The asssessment will identify which watersheds are important and for what purposes (in a spatially explicit format), for more than 80 percent of national forest lands in the four regions.

Recent strategies for national forests have focused on restoring the natural ecological processes that will create and maintain diverse and resilient aquatic habitat (Northwest Forest Plan, Tongass National Forest, PACFISH; proposed for the Sierra Nevada provinces and the Interior Columbia Basin.) These efforts will move east and probably be incorporated into revised forest plans in the next several years. ❖

Integrating Watersheds from the Headwaters Through the Cities

National forests typically occupy the head-waters of large river basins. Forest activities affect the water resource; so do downstream land uses. In general, watersheds on the national forests are in relatively good shape compared to soils, waters, and riparian areas on private lands, ranches, and farms, and urban areas that typically occupy the lower parts of a large river basin. It will take a comprehensive, watershed approach to improve water quality or restore the full range of watershed function to the system.

Water quality problems, and solutions, are disproportionately tied to urban areas. Urban areas are often forested and make a major contribution to maintaining and improving water quality. Counties classified as "urban" now contain one-quarter of the total tree cover of the coterminous United States.

Urban trees affect the volume of runoff by intercepting precipitation, slowing water infiltration rates, and transpiring water. By intercepting and retaining or slowing the flow of precipitation reaching the ground, trees (in conjunction with soils) play an important role in urban hydrologic processes. They can reduce the rate and volume of storm water runoff, flooding damage, stormwater treatment costs, and other problems related to water quality. Estimates of runoff for an intensive storm in Dayton, OH, showed that the existing tree canopy (22 percent) reduced potential runoff by 7 percent and that a modest increase in canopy cover (29 percent) would reduce runoff by nearly 12 percent (Sanders 1986). A study of the Gwynns Falls watershed in Baltimore indicated that heavy forest cover can reduce total runoff by as much as 26 percent and increase low-flow runoff by up to 13 percent, compared with treeless areas, for equivalent land-use conditions (Neville 1996). Tree cover over pervious surfaces reduced total runoff by as much as 40 percent; tree canopy cover over impervious surfaces had a limited effect on runoff. In reducing runoff, trees function like retention structures. In many communities, reduced runoff from rainfall interception can also reduce costs of treating stormwater by decreasing the volume of water handled during periods of peak runoff (Sanders 1986).

Hydrologic costs may also be associated with urban vegetation, particularly in arid environments where water is increasingly scarce. Increased water use in desert regions could alter the local water balance and various ecosystem functions tied to the desert water cycle. In addition, annual costs of water for sustaining vegetation can be twice as great as energy savings from shade for tree species that use large amounts of water, such as mulberry (McPherson and Dougherty 1989). In Tucson, AZ, 16 percent of the annual irrigation requirement of trees was offset by the amount of water conserved at power plants because of the energy savings from trees (Dwyer et al. 1992).

Urban waterways are strongly influenced by impervious surfaces that generate large volumes of rapid surface runoff, contaminants, and thermal loads. The effects of temperature extremes, nutrient loading, toxins, bed instability, current velocities, and disturbance frequencies are all magnified in urban watersheds. Urban vegetation can reduce many of these adverse effects by cooling air temperatures, shading waterways, removing pollutants from both water and air, reducing surface and subsurface flows, and by reducing pollutant emissions from various sources (Nowak et al. 1998).

POLICY IMPLICATIONS

Research is critically needed that integrates these numerous vegetation effects to evaluate the total effects of urban vegetation and various vegetation designs on water quantity and quality. This research should include field measurements, computer modeling, and model validation. The Baltimore long-term ecosystem research project is currently investigating and integrating many of these research issues to help answer this complex question. More research and field measurements are needed to determine appropriate urban vegetation management strategies and designs to improve water and stream quality in and around urban areas, and consequently improve human health and environmental quality in the Nation. ❖

Next Steps

*T*his report contains information that can be used to help articulate and guide the agency's commitment to watershed health and restoration. The report is a first step in identifying the particular role of national forests in providing water to the Nation and restoring watersheds to a healthy, sustainable functioning condition

The report has focused on answering basic questions about the quantity, quality, uses, and value of waters that flow from the national forests; about the condition and trend of national forest watersheds; and about strategies for protecting and restoring degraded waters and watersheds. We have surveyed the published information and tried to capture the current state of our understanding in this paper—though in sharply condensed form. Along the way, we have noted gaps in the data and questions particularly ripe for further inquiry. Action items for additional investigation include:

■ Refine water-yield estimates to the national forest scale. Precision estimates by forest and State are necessary to drive water valuation models and aid in revising forest plans. This action could be completed in 6 to 12 months, with a term or post-doctoral position.

■ Refine our estimate of the value of water on and flowing from national forest lands. The estimate of the value of water from national forest lands in this paper is a first approximation that does not include dilution, navigation, quality of water, and nonuse values nor does it estimate the value of careful forest management in sustaining a watershed's ability to store and distribute water and moderate downstream flooding.

■ Convene a leadership forum to examine the particular role that the Forest Service plays in providing clean water to the Nation and determine the kinds of watershed and forest management programs that will maintain long-term, high-quality water and keep national forest watersheds operating within their historical range of variability.

■ Develop and activate a communications strategy on the connection of forested watersheds and clean water in urban settings, addressed to urban and suburban publics and policymakers. This strategy would highlight the contributions that national forest lands, technical assistance, and stewardship programs can make to water quality, reduced storm runoff, drought reduction, and watershed health.

■ Complete an agency-wide assessment of special-emphasis and biodiversity watersheds, modeled on the assessment work of the Inland West Water Institute.

In the meantime, the Forest Service is actively pursuing initiatives to restore watersheds, improve water quality, and protect aquatic habitats. The Chief has made watershed health and restoration, recreation, sustainable forestry, and roads management the agency's top priorities. The Committee of Scientists recommended that the Secretary of Agriculture highlight the need to plan for conserving and restoring watersheds through maintaining flow regimes. These efforts recognize that watershed integrity will be maintained and restored, in part, through sustainable management of the national forests. But watersheds are larger than forests, watershed health will be achieved only through collaborative partnership efforts at the watershed scale as envisioned in the Clean Water Action Plan headed by the Administrator of the EPA and Secretary of Agriculture. The Forest Service has a vital role to play on both sides of the national forest boundaries.

The challenge for watershed-based approaches will be to develop a shared vision for healthy and productive watersheds, based on understanding natural and human-induced variability at scales ranging from small (<20,000 acre) to large (>1,000,000 acre). New strategies are needed for managing in mixed-ownership watersheds, as well as creating new partnerships for effective learning, assimilating new knowledge, and implementing our shared vision. ❖

References

Brown, T. 1999. Notes on the Economic Value of Water from National Forests. Unpublished report. USDA Forest Service, Rocky Mountain Research Station. Fort Collins, CO.

Coleman, E.A. 1953. Vegetation and Watershed Management. The Ronald Press.

Croft, A.R. and Bailey, Reed W. May 1964. Mountain Water. USDA Forest Service, Intermountain Region, Ogden, UT

Dwyer, J.F., Nowak, D.J., Noble, M.H., and Sisini, S.M. (in press). Connecting People with Ecosystems in the 21st Century: An Assessment of our Nation's Urban Forests (PNW GTR xxx): U.S. Department of Agriculture, Forest Service. Pacific Northwest Research Station. Portland, OR.

Forest Ecosystem Management Assessment Team: An Ecological, Economic, and Social Assessment Report of the Forest Ecosystem Management Assessment Team (FEMAT) 1993.

Frederick, K. D. and Sedjo, R. A. 1991. America's Renewable Resources: Historical Trends and Current Challenges. Resources for the Future, Washington, DC.

Frederick, K. D. 1991. Water Resources: Increasing Demand and Scarce Supplies. In: America's Renewable Resources: Historical Trends and Current Challenges, Kenneth D. Frederick and Roger A. Sedjo, eds., Resources for the Future, Washington, DC.

Gillian, D.M. and Brown, T.C. 1997. Instream flow protection: Seeking a balance in western water use. Island Press, Washington, DC.

Gleick, P. H. 1993. Water in Crisis: A Guide to the World's Fresh Water Resources. Oxford University, Oxford.

Gleick, P. H. 1998. The World's Water: The Biennial Report on Freshwater Resources. Island Press. Washington, DC.

Graf, W.L. 1999. Downstream Geomorphic Impacts of Large Dams on American Rivers. Arizona State University, Department of Geography, Tempe, AZ. (unpublished manuscript).

Hansen, T. and Hallum, A. 1990. Water allocation tradeoffs: Irrigation and recreation. Agricultural Economic Report number 634, Resources and Technology Division. Economic Research Service, U.S. Department of Agriculture.

Hann, W.J., Jones, J.L. Karl, M.G. [et al.] 1997. Landscape dynamics of the basin. In Quigley, T.M.: Arbelbide, S.J., (tech. eds.). An assessment of ecosystem components in the interior Columbia Basin and portions of the Klamath and Great Basins. Gen. Tech. Rep. PNW-GTR-405, Chapter 3. U.S. Department of Agriculture, Forest Service, Pacific Northwest Research Station. Portland, OR.

Harr, R. D. 1983. Potential for Augmenting Water Yield Through Forest Practices in Western Washington and Western Oregon. Water Resources Bulletin 19(3):383-394.

Kattelmann, R. C., Berg, N. H., and Rector, J. 1983. The Potential for Increasing Streamflow from Sierra Nevada Watersheds. Water Resources Bulletin 19(3):395-402.

MacCleery, D. W. 1992. American Forests: A History of Resiliency and Recovery. USDA Forest Service, FS-540, in cooperation with the Forest History Society, Durham, NC.

McPherson, E.G. and Dougherty, E. 1989. Selecting trees for shade in the Southwest, J. Arboriculture 15:35-43.

Modeling the effects of urban vegetation on air pollution, In: Air Pollution Modeling and Its Application XII. (S. Gryning and N. Chaumerliac, eds.) Plenum Press, New York, pp. 399-407.

Neville, L.R. 1996. Urban Watershed Management: the Role of Vegetation. Ph.D. dissertation. SUNY College of Environmental Science and Forestry, Syracuse, NY.

Moody, D.W. 1990. Groundwater contamination in the United States. Journal of Soil and Water Conservation 45: 170-179.

National Research Council. 1992. Restoration of aquatic ecosystems. National Academy Press, Washington, DC.

The Nature Conservancy. 1996. Aquatic/Wetland Species at Risk Map. in: The Index of Watershed Indicators, U.S. EPA. EPA-841-R-97-010, September 1997. p. 22

Neilson, Ronald. 1995. A model for predicting continental-scale vegetation distribution and water balance. Ecological Applications 5(2):362-385.

Noble, E. 1965. Sediment Reduction through Watershed Rehabilitation. USDA Agricultural Research Service, Washington DC. Paper 18, Interagency Sedimentation Conference 1963, p. 114-123. In: Proc. Fed. Misc. Pub. 970

Nowak, D.J., Civerolo, K.L., Rao, S.T., Sistla, G., Luley, C.J., and Crane, D.E., in review. The impact of urban trees on ozone in the Northeastern United States. Atmos. Env.

Pinchot, G. 1947. Breaking New Ground. Harcourt and Brace, New York.

Rodgers, A. D. III. 1991. Bernard Eduard Fernow: A story of North American Forestry. Forest History Society, Durham, NC.

References

Sanders, R.A. 1986. Urban vegetation impacts on the urban hydrology of Dayton Ohio. Urban Ecology 9:361-376.

Schmidt, L. J. and Solomon, R.M. 1981. The National Forest Role in Augmenting the Drop of Water. In: Arizona Water Symposium 25th Annual Proceedings. Arizona Department of Water Resources. Report #3.

Shiklomanov, I. A. 1993. World Fresh Water Resources. In: Water in Crisis: A Guide to the World's Fresh Water Resources. Oxford University Press. Oxford.

Solley, W. B., Pierce, R., Perlman, H. 1998. Estimated use of water in the United States. In: 1995 U.S. Geological Survey. Circular 1200, Denver, CO.

Souch, C.A. and Souch, C. 1993, The effect of trees on summertime below canopy urban climates: a case study, Bloomington, Indiana. J. Arboric. 19(5):303-312.

Steen, H. K. 1991. The Beginning of the National Forest System. FS-488, USDA Forest Service. Washington DC

Taha, H. 1996. Modeling impacts of increased urban vegetation on ozone air quality in the South Coast Air Basin, Atmos. Env. 30(20):3,423-3,430.

Tongass National Forest, Land and Resource Management Plan, Record of Decision, signed April 12, 1999.

USDA Forest Service. 1998. Land Areas of the National Forest System, 1997. FS-383. Washington, DC.

USDA Forest Service. 1999. Roads Analysis: Informing Decisions About Managing the National Forest Transportation System. FS-643. Washington, DC.

U.S. Water Resources Council. 1978. The Nation's Water Resources 1975-2000. Washington, DC: Government Printing Office.

U.S. Water Resources Council, Second National Water Assessment, Vol. I: Summary, 052-045-00051-7, Washington, DC: Government Printing Office, 1978. pp. 20, 21.

Ziemer, R. 1987. Water Yields from Forests: An Agnostic View. In: R.Z. Callaham and J.J. DeVries (Tech. Coord.) Proceedings of the California Watershed Management Conference, November 18-20, 1986, West Sacramento, CA. 74-78. Wildland Resources Center, University of California, Berkeley CA. Report 11, Feb. 1982.